# Six Plays Today

**Paul Groves**
Head of English
St Hugh's Church of England Comprehensive School
Grantham

**Nigel Grimshaw**
Formerly Senior Lecturer in English
Kesteven College of Education
Peterborough

```
LOXLEY HALL SCHOOL
   STAFFORD ROAD
     UTTOXETER
       STAFFS
      ST14 8RS
    01889 562388
```

John Murray

# Contents

| | |
|---|---:|
| A Weekend Away | 1 |
| Meeting Mr West | 14 |
| You, the Jury | 27 |
| Home Sweet Home | 34 |
| Neighbours | 43 |
| The Shelter | 52 |

# A Weekend Away

Miss Bell
Miss Ward
Mr Blake
Mr Kirk
Dave Dunston
Tim Frost
Errol Constantine
Vicky Walker
Lynn Norton
Mina Desai
Ben Charlton
Cliff Gates

## Scene 1

(*A large room in an old house. The house belongs to an education authority. It is used as a centre for residential courses and adventure weekends for young people.*
*The room itself is a dining area. Three doors can be seen. One leads to the kitchen, the next to the sleeping area and the third leads to an outer door.*
**Miss Bell** *comes in with the school party. For a moment, they stand looking round. Most of them are carrying rucksacks or bags and they put these down.*)

**Vicky**  Did you notice those people back in the village?
**Ben**  No.
**Vicky**  Outside the shop. They all stared as we drove past.
**Mina**  Cheeky lot.

1

**Miss Bell**  They were probably wondering if you were St Jude's coming back. So you'd better behave yourselves.
**Vicky**  Who are St Jude's?
**Miss Bell**  Another school party who stayed here a week or two ago. They were terrors by all accounts.
**Mina**  What did they do?
**Miss Bell**  I don't know exactly. But they left a lot of bad feeling behind.
**Lynn**  There was a fierce-looking man in the lane outside. He was staring, too.

(**Miss Ward** *comes in*)

**Miss Bell**  He looked like a gamekeeper to me.
**Mina**  What does a gamekeeper do?
**Miss Ward**  He looks after pheasants and other game.
**Cliff**  I always thought birds and wild animals looked after themselves.
**Miss Ward**  Well, we learn something new every day, Gates, don't we?
**Errol**  (*to* **Ben**) What a dump!
**Lynn**  We don't sleep here, miss, do we?
**Miss Ward**  Don't be silly. This is the dining area. Can't you see?
**Vicky**  Bit grim, isn't it?
**Miss Ward**  What did you expect on a weekend like this — a first-class hotel?
**Lynn**  Please, miss ——
**Errol**  When can we start getting some grub ready, miss?
**Miss Ward**  In a minute. Miss Bell and I will deal with that.
**Lynn**  I don't feel well, miss.
**Miss Bell**  Probably the long drive in the minibus. You'll feel better soon.
**Ben**  How about getting the rest of the stuff out of the bus, miss?
**Miss Ward**  Mr Blake is organising that. Don't worry.
**Lynn**  I do feel bad, miss.
**Miss Bell**  We'll sort out the sleeping arrangements. Then she can lie down.
**Lynn**  I think I'd better go home, miss.

**Miss Ward**  But you can't go home, girl. It's over a hundred miles away.
**Lynn**  I want to, miss. I don't feel well.
**Miss Ward**  Out of the question.
**Miss Bell**  We'll make a drink in a minute or two. You'll feel better after that.

(**Mr Blake** *comes in*)

**Mr Blake**  Are Dunston and Frost in here?
**Miss Ward**  No. They should be outside, helping you.
**Mr Blake**  They must have cleared off while I was parking the bus.
**Vicky**  Typical.
**Mr Blake**  Right. Charlton, Constantine — and you, Gates — come with me.
**Cliff**  I'm not supposed to do heavy lifting, sir.
**Mr Blake**  Oh, yes, you are. Come on.

(**Mr Blake** *goes out. The boys follow*)

**Miss Ward**  We'll sort out the bedrooms for you girls.
**Miss Bell**  It's this way, I think.

(**Miss Bell** *leads the way, followed by the others*)

**Mina**  I hope we're not going to be sleeping on straw.
**Lynn**  Oh, no! We couldn't be, could we?

(*The room is empty for a moment. Then* **Dave Dunston** *and* **Tim Frost** *rush in, panting*)

**Dave**  Do you think he'll follow us?
**Tim**  I think he missed us in the trees.
**Dave**  He had a gun, you know.
**Tim**  It was a stick.
**Dave**  It was a flipping gun, mate!
**Tim**  Shut up! Someone's coming.

(**Mr Blake** *and the other three boys come in, carrying rucksacks and cardboard boxes which they put down*)

**Mr Blake**  Where have you two been?
**Tim**  Just outside, sir.

**Mr Blake**  Dodging work, eh? Well, now you're here, start stacking all this gear against that wall.

(**Ben** and **Errol** go out. **Cliff** lingers)

**Dave**  (picking up two rucksacks) Over there, sir?
**Tim**  (lifting a cardboard box) Righto, sir!

(Near the wall **Tim** trips and drops the box)

**Mr Blake**  Careful!
**Tim**  Sorry, sir.

(There is a loud knocking at the outer door)

**Mr Blake**  See who that is, someone.

(**Cliff** goes out. **Ben** and **Errol**, carrying boxes and rucksacks, come in)

**Ben**  This is the last of it, sir.
**Mr Blake**  Good. Put it with the rest. We'll sort it all out later.

(**Mr Kirk** comes in, followed by **Cliff**)

**Mr Kirk**  Are you in charge here?
**Mr Blake**  I'm one of the people in charge. What's the trouble?
**Mr Kirk**  Two of your lot have been trespassing and causing damage.
**Mr Blake**  Are you sure? We've only just arrived.
**Mr Kirk**  Of course I'm sure.
**Mr Blake**  What sort of damage?
**Mr Kirk**  I saw them in the woods. They were scaring the pheasants.
**Mr Blake**  Right, Mr — er —
**Mr Kirk**  Kirk's the name — gamekeeper.
**Mr Blake**  Well, Mr Kirk, if you're sure, I'll find out who they were and deal with them.
**Mr Kirk**  I should hope so. I'm getting sick and tired of these school parties rampaging round up here. So are most people.
**Mr Blake**  You can't blame us for what other parties may have done. It's our first visit here.

**Mr Kirk** These kids from the cities — they're all the same.
**Mr Blake** I know you've had a bit of trouble from one school that came here. It doesn't mean that all children are alike.
**Mr Kirk** A bit of trouble? You don't know the half of it. Little devils!
**Mr Blake** You won't be troubled by that kind of behaviour from this party, Mr Kirk.
**Mr Kirk** Won't I? What about those two I just saw?
**Mr Blake** I'll put a stop to it, Mr Kirk. I've just said so.
**Mr Kirk** Well — see that you do.
**Mr Blake** I will.
**Mr Kirk** (*scowls at them all for a moment*) That's it, then. Keep an eye on them and we'll have no bother.

(**Mr Kirk** *goes out*)

**Mr Blake** Dunston! Frost! What did you think you were playing at?
**Tim** We weren't doing any harm, sir.
**Dave** Frostie thought he saw a badger, sir.
**Tim** We climbed over the fence to have a look.
**Dave** We didn't go far into the wood.
**Mr Blake** Did you damage any trees? Chase any pheasants?
**Tim** No, sir. Honest, sir. We were just looking.
**Dave** Then he came rushing up, shouting.
**Mr Blake** Well, keep out of there. All of you!
**Errol** Why are you getting at us, sir?
**Cliff** We've done nothing.
**Ben** It was Dunston and Frost.
**Errol** They're always doing something daft.
**Tim** No, we're not.
**Cliff** Yes, you are.
**Mr Blake** That's enough. (*to* **Dunston** *and* **Frost**) I'll make sure you two have enough to do during the rest of our stay to keep you out of mischief.
**Dave** We were only looking, sir.
**Mr Blake** You were trespassing. (*to* **Ben**) The minibus is empty, is it?
**Ben** Yes, sir.

**Mr Blake**   Good. Let's sort out the sleeping arrangements, then. This way.

(**Mr Blake** *leads the way out to the bedrooms and the others follow*)

**Scene 2**

(*Some time later.* **Miss Ward, Miss Bell** *and the girls are standing near the cardboard boxes.* **Ben** *comes out of the kitchen. He has an armful of old newspapers and empty cartons*)

**Miss Ward**   We're getting things sorted out at last.
**Ben**   That's cleared up the kitchen, miss.

(**Ben** *goes out through the door that leads outside*)

**Miss Bell**   That St Jude's party must have run wild.
**Vicky**   They really left that kitchen in a mess, didn't they?
**Mina**   It was full of rubbish scattered everywhere, miss!
**Lynn**   There were empty packets and tins and paper!
**Mina**   All over the floor!
**Miss Ward**   It's clear now. So we can start moving the food boxes in there.
**Miss Bell**   You should be able to carry one each.
**Vicky**   (*picks one up and looks inside*) There's all bits of egg-shell and slime on top of this one.

(**Cliff** *comes in and stands watching them*)

**Miss Ward**   Just carry it into the kitchen, Vicky.
**Miss Bell**   Unload it in there. Then you can clean up the other things in the box.
**Mina**   (*peering into* **Vicky's** *box*) There must be half a dozen eggs in there, all smashed.
**Miss Ward**   Yes, Mina. That's why Mr Blake has gone down to the village for some more.
**Lynn**   I wonder how they got broken.
**Cliff**   It was Frostie. He dropped the box. I saw him.
**Vicky**   He's always doing things like that. So is Dunston.
**Miss Ward**   I'd better go and see what they're doing.

6

(**Ben** *comes in*)

**Cliff**  We couldn't put the rubbish in the bins, miss. They were all full.
**Miss Ward**  Oh? What did you do with it?
**Ben**  We just piled it up, miss.
**Miss Bell**  I hope you weighted it down with stones. It's windy out there.
**Miss Ward**  Yes. We don't want it blowing about all over the place.

(**Errol** *comes in*)

**Errol**  They're burning the rubbish, miss.
**Miss Ward**  They're what?
**Errol**  Burning it, miss. And there are bits of blazing paper blowing everywhere!
**Miss Ward**  Oh, Lord! Don't they know that's dangerous?

(**Miss Ward** *is going out when* **Mr Kirk** *comes in with* **Dunston** *and* **Frost**)

**Mr Kirk**  Where's the teacher?
**Miss Ward**  We're teachers.
**Mr Kirk**  You? Where's the man?
**Miss Bell**  He's in the village.
**Mr Kirk**  Left you to look after things, eh? I might have known. Two women!
**Miss Ward**  What do you mean?
**Mr Kirk**  I told him to keep an eye on this lot. Next thing I find is that they're lighting fires all over the countryside.
**Tim**  We were only trying to burn a bit of rubbish.
**Mr Kirk**  There hasn't been any rain for a week. With that wind they could have had the woods on fire.
**Miss Ward**  I'm afraid they weren't thinking. They'd cleared out a lot of rubbish from here. Then they found the dustbins were full. I'm sorry.
**Mr Kirk**  Sorry? Oh yes. The last lot were very sorry, too. A serious complaint has gone in about that school. And I'm going to send in another letter about your lot.
**Miss Ward**  That's a bit extreme.
**Miss Bell**  Is that really fair?

7

**Mr Kirk** I'm not standing here arguing. I've got better things to do. Keep these kids in order, or else!

(**Mr Kirk** *goes out*)

**Miss Ward** (*to* **Dunston** *and* **Frost**) Why don't you two ever think? Come with me. Let's see what you've been up to.

(**Miss Ward** *goes out and the two boys follow*)

**Miss Bell** The rest of you — get these boxes into the kitchen. I could do with a cup of tea.

(**Miss Bell** *and the children, carrying boxes, go out into the kitchen*)

## Scene 3

(*The same room some time later. The teachers and* **Vicky, Lynn, Mina** *and* **Cliff** *are there*)

**Miss Bell** Well, at least we managed to have a meal.
**Miss Ward** And Dunston and Frost are washing up.
**Miss Bell** They can't get into much trouble in the kitchen.
**Mr Blake** Don't bet on it.

(**Ben** *and* **Errol** *come in*)

**Ben** We've crammed some of the rubbish into the bins, sir.
**Errol** And weighted the rest down with stones. It won't blow about.
**Mr Blake** Good. Now you're all here, I want to talk to you.
**Mina** What about, sir? *We* haven't done anything wrong.
**Vicky** You can't blame us for Dunston and Frost, sir.
**Cliff** It's that man. He's got it in for us.
**Ben** He's the one who's giving us a bad name.
**Lynn** He's going to write a letter about us.
**Mr Blake** I know. I'll go and see him tomorrow. He may have calmed down by then.
**Miss Bell** He certainly wouldn't listen to sense tonight.
**Mr Blake** No. Now — these are some points to watch while we're staying here ——

(**Mr Kirk** *comes in quietly. They turn and look at him*)

**Mr Blake**  Lord! What now?
**Mr Kirk**  Could I use your phone?
**Mr Blake**  Of course. What's wrong?
**Mr Kirk**  A front tyre on the car burst. I swerved off the road into a ditch.
**Mr Blake**  We can help you to get it out. There are enough of us here.
**Mr Kirk**  Er — no. No, thank you. Only — could one of the young ladies go and sit with my wife? I left her in the car.
**Miss Ward**  Is she hurt?
**Mr Kirk**  No. Just a bit upset. But she's been ill for some time. I was taking her down to the doctor. He wanted to see her and she needs some more pills.
**Mr Blake**  Can she walk?
**Mr Kirk**  Oh, yes. But she's a bit shaken up. She'll be all right if she can get some more pills.
**Mr Blake**  Then don't bother about the phone. Come on. (*He takes* **Mr Kirk's** *arm*)
**Mr Kirk**  Where?
**Mr Blake**  I'll run you and your wife down to the doctor in the minibus. You can get your car out later.
**Mr Kirk**  Oh, I don't know that I could —
**Mr Blake**  Come on. No bother. Don't let's waste any more time.

(**Mr Blake** *takes* **Mr Kirk** *out*)

**Miss Bell**  Poor man.
**Miss Ward**  He's certainly had to change his tune from last time.
**Lynn**  Will his wife die, miss?
**Miss Ward**  You are a little ray of sunshine, Lynn, aren't you? I shouldn't think so.
**Vicky**  Serves him right.
**Mina**  Don't be so mean, Vicky. He could have hurt himself.
**Miss Ward**  I've got an idea. He's obviously a man who doesn't think much of women and children. We'll heap coals of fire on his head.

**Errol**  You can't do that, miss.
**Cliff**  They'll put us in prison.
**Miss Bell**  'Heaping coals of fire' is a way of saying you're going to return good for evil.
**Ben**  How?
**Miss Ward**  You'll see. Get Dunston and Frost from the kitchen.
**Ben**  (*going to the kitchen door*) Come on, you two. You're wanted.
**Miss Ward**  All of you – outside.
**Cliff**  What's she going to do?
**Errol**  Why ask me?

(**Miss Ward** *goes out followed by the others and by* **Dunston** *and* **Frost** *who come out of the kitchen*)

## Scene 4

(*The same room some time later. All the teachers, all the children and* **Mr Kirk** *are there*)

**Mr Kirk**  There's hardly a scratch on my car. How did you get it back on the road?
**Errol**  We all pushed it.
**Cliff**  It wasn't half heavy.
**Ben**  Get away, Cliff! All you did was lean on it.
**Mr Kirk**  And who changed the wheel?
**Miss Ward**  I did. Dunston helped.
**Mr Kirk**  Who's Dunston?
**Dave**  I am.
**Mr Kirk**  Oh. I don't know what to say.
**Mr Blake**  Don't say anything, Mr Kirk. You'd better get home and look after Mrs Kirk.
**Mr Kirk**  I feel a fool. I shouldn't have carried on at you the way I did.
**Miss Bell**  You must have been worrying about Mrs Kirk. We understand.
**Mr Kirk**  Giving me a lift down to the village, waiting at the doctor's and running me and Mrs Kirk home. Bringing me back to the car. And then to find that you'd got it back on

the road and changed the wheel. I don't know how to thank you.

**Miss Ward**   Don't worry about it.

**Mr Kirk**   After this — anything you want to know — anything you want — come to me.

**Mr Blake**   We will.

**Mr Kirk**   I'm really lost for words. I'll come back in the morning. And thank you. Thank you all very much.

**Mr Blake**   That's quite all right. You can run yourself home, can't you?

**Mr Kirk**   Oh yes, of course, Thanks again. Thanks a lot.

(**Mr Kirk** *goes out*)

**Dave**   Do we still have to finish that washing up, miss?

**Miss Ward**   Yes. It'll keep you out of harm's way. Get on with it.

**Tim**   Come on, mate.

(**Tim** *and* **Dave** *go out to the kitchen*)

**Vicky**   What are we going to do tomorrow, sir?

**Mr Blake**   Give us a chance, Vicky. We haven't got today over yet.

**Miss Bell**   Still — all's well that ends well.

**Miss Ward**   Yes, we can all relax a bit now.

**Miss Bell**   Lynn — I'm sorry. In all the rush we forgot about you.

**Lynn**   About what, miss?

**Miss Bell**   You weren't feeling well. Do you want an aspirin? I've got some here.

**Lynn**   Oh no, miss. I'm fine. I like it here now. It's exciting.

**Mr Blake**   Exciting! I could think of another word.

(**Tim** *comes in*)

**Tim**   Dunston's just dropped four plates, miss, and broken them.

**Mr Blake**   Don't put those aspirins away, Miss Bell. I can feel a slight headache coming on.

## The people in the play

1 Which of the boys seems most helpful to the teachers?
2 About how old are the children? Are they all of the same age or are some older than others? Give some reasons for your answer.
3 Which of the teachers seems most kind-hearted? Say why you think so.
4 Is Lynn really ill at the beginning of the play or not? Use some evidence from the play to show why you think as you do.
5 What is your judgement of Mr Kirk? Is he just a bad-tempered man or has he some excuse for the way he talks about the children? In one or two sentences write what you think of him.
6 Are Dave Dunston and Tim Frost stupid or just unlucky or even trying to be clever? Give your opinion of them in a sentence or two.
7 What is your opinion of Cliff Gates? Say why you think of him as you do.
8 In scene 3, just before Mr Kirk comes in, what do you think Mr Blake is going to talk to the group about?
9 In what way do Miss Ward, Miss Bell and the others 'heap coals of fire' on Mr Kirk's head?
10 At the end Miss Ward makes Dunston and Frost finish the washing up. This is a kind of punishment. Is it fair? Do they deserve more? Or less? Should they have been punished at all? What do you think?
11 What do you think has given Mr Blake his headache at the end of the play?

## Town and country

1 If you were a farmer, what sort of things would you dislike visitors to the country doing? List some of them.
2 Which place do you prefer, the country or a town? Write about some of the things you enjoy in the country or, if you don't like the country, write about your dislikes.
3 Should people who don't live in the country be allowed to go

only into special parts of it such as parks and some nature reserves? Or should they be allowed to go anywhere they like — into forestry plantations or across farmland for instance? Explain why you think as you do.

## Writing

1 The teachers and the children go out the next day to a nearby large town. They might visit a museum or an old castle or go for a walk round the town walls. Does anything happen to Dunston and Frost? Perhaps someone gets lost. Does one of the party complain a lot? You can write a whole play or a scene from it. Set out your work in the same way as this play. You can bring in other characters such as people the children might meet in the town.

2 The school party go for a walk on the moors. Perhaps the weather turns bad. Does it rain hard? How do they all react to getting wet? Or perhaps a fog comes down and they lose their way. Someone might sprain an ankle. Could it be Mr Blake? How do they get that person home? Write a whole play or a scene from it. Set out your work in the same way as this play.

3 Why did the party from St Jude's leave such a bad reputation behind them? Write a short account of some of the things they might have done.

4 Some local people said that the party from St Jude's behaved badly because they were allowed to get away with it. Do people only behave well because they are afraid of being punished if they don't? Do you? Or do you believe that people should behave well and be considerate anyway? Write your opinion, giving some examples from your own experience to show why you think as you do.

Perhaps you can discuss this last question as a class or as a group.

# Meeting Mr West

**Gran** (*Mrs Dawson's mother*)
**Mrs Jane Dawson**
**Jill Dawson**
**Keith Dawson**
**Greg Southern**
**Russell Dale**
**Mr Bill West**

## Scene 1

(*The living room of the Dawsons' house.* **Gran** *and* **Mrs Dawson** *are there*)

**Gran**  Can't you ring him and put him off? You'll see him at work tomorrow.
**Mrs Dawson**  No. I've tried again and again to arrange for you all to meet him. It's just never worked out. Tonight he's coming.
**Gran**  I warned you earlier I wasn't feeling well.
**Mrs Dawson**  You could always go up to bed.
**Gran**  It's cold up there.
**Mrs Dawson**  You'll feel better in the morning. Put the electric fire on and I'll bring you up a hotwater bottle. I've got time before I go down to the station to meet him.
**Gran**  You're not going to leave me here all on my own, are you? Why do you have to pick him up?
**Mrs Dawson**  His car's in for repair. And you won't be left on your own. The children will be here.
**Gran**  I'd have thought that after John walked out on you, you

would have had enough of men to last you a lifetime.
**Mrs Dawson**  Bill isn't anything like John.
**Gran**  I don't want him here tonight.
**Mrs Dawson**  You've made that very clear.
**Gran**  And don't start being short with me.
**Mrs Dawson**  I wasn't.
**Gran**  I speak my mind, I do.
**Mrs Dawson**  I know. Why don't you just go and lie down?

(**Keith** *comes in*)

**Keith**  Mum! Where's my bomber jacket?
**Mrs Dawson**  Where you left it, I suppose.
**Keith**  No, it isn't.
**Gran**  You should look after your things. I had to when I was your age.
**Mrs Dawson**  When did you last have it?
**Keith**  I don't know. Where did you put it? I'm going out.
**Mrs Dawson**  You're not. Mr West's coming. I told you.
**Keith**  Oh, Mum! I've got to go out. Russ is calling for me.
**Mrs Dawson**  You're staying here to meet Mr West.

(**Jill** *comes in*)

**Jill**  I shan't be able to stop in tonight, Mum. I'm sorry.
**Mrs Dawson**  Jill! You've got to be in tonight. Mr West wants to meet you all.
**Jill**  I must meet Greg. He phoned me at the office this afternoon.
**Mrs Dawson**  Greg!
**Jill**  Yes, Mum — Greg!
**Mrs Dawson**  Now just listen to me — both of you! I told you Mr West was coming. You know this evening's important to me. I left work early to get things ready. Now you say you're going out. Well — you can't.
**Jill**  Mum! It's you he's coming to see.
**Gran**  Selfish! That's what you are, young lady.
**Jill**  You keep out of it.
**Gran**  Don't you talk to me like that.
**Mrs Dawson**  Jill! You can't let me down — not for Greg. You swore you'd finished with him.

**Jill** Well, I haven't.
**Mrs Dawson** You're a fool. You can't rely on a word he says.
**Jill** You don't know anything about him, Mum.
**Mrs Dawson** I know he's a married man with two children. You told me so yourself.
**Jill** He's not married. They're separated.
**Mrs Dawson** Anyway, see him another night, if you must. I want you here at home tonight.
**Jill** I'm sorry. He'll be waiting for me now.
**Mrs Dawson** But you can't be so rude. What will Mr West think? He's coming specially to meet you.
**Jill** I can't help that.
**Mrs Dawson** You're not going!
**Jill** Yes, I am.

(*The door bell rings*)

**Keith** That'll be Russ. I'll go.
**Mrs Dawson** Tell him you can't come out.
**Keith** His cousin's got a new trail bike. We're going to try it out.
**Mrs Dawson** You can try it another night.
**Keith** Oh, Mum!

(**Keith** *goes out*)

**Jill** I'm late.
**Mrs Dawson** Jill!
**Jill** Sorry, Mum. I'll try and get back early.

(**Jill** *goes out*)

**Gran** You're too soft with them both. Stop her.
**Mrs Dawson** How can I? I can't go out in the street and drag her back, can I?
**Gran** They're like their father. He was like that all the time. Self, self, self — that's all they think about.
**Mrs Dawson** Oh, don't start, mother. I'd planned this evening. I wanted Bill to meet the children — to meet you. I wanted him to get to know you all.
**Gran** I can't meet him. I feel terrible. I'll have to go to bed.
**Mrs Dawson** All right, mother.

**Gran**  I can't manage on my own. You'll have to help me.
**Mrs Dawson**  Oh, mother!
**Gran**  I'm ill, I tell you. Take me upstairs.
**Mrs Dawson**  Come on, then. Lean on me.

(**Mrs Dawson** *helps* **Gran** *through the door. The room is empty for a moment. Then* **Keith** *comes in with* **Russ**)

**Keith**  Mum?
**Russ**  She must have gone out.
**Keith**  She said she was going to the station to meet someone.
**Russ**  This visitor you're having?
**Keith**  Yes.
**Russ**  And you've got to stay in because of him.
**Keith**  Yes.
**Russ**  That's a bit rough. You know what Geoff's like. He won't let us have a go on his bike any time we want.
**Keith**  I know. He might not give us another go.
**Russ**  How long do you reckon your Mum will be gone?
**Keith**  Half an hour. Maybe more.
**Russ**  You could come out for that long.
**Keith**  Hey! Or even an hour. I don't have to spend the whole evening talking to him and Mum, do I?
**Russ**  Why are we wasting time here, then?
**Keith**  Right. Let's go.

(**Keith** *and* **Russ** *hurry out. After a moment,* **Mrs Dawson** *comes back into the room*)

**Mrs Dawson**  Keith? (*She goes back to the door and calls through it*) Keith! (*She waits and comes back into the middle of the room*) He's gone. The little devil. And I'm going to be late for the train.

(**Mrs Dawson** *goes out*)

17

# Scene 2

(*The same room some time later.* **Bill West** *and* **Mrs Dawson** *are sitting talking*)

**Mrs Dawson**  I just can't get over it. They knew you were coming tonight and they knew why.
**Bill West**  Let's forget it for now, Jane. There'll be other times.
**Mrs Dawson**  But why tonight? Why did they all have to disappear tonight of all nights?
**Bill**  Jealousy, do you think?
**Mrs Dawson**  Jealousy?
**Bill**  They know we're thinking of getting married. They don't want to share you with anyone.
**Mrs Dawson**  But that's silly.
**Bill**  It's only a thought.

(**Gran** *comes in, carrying a hotwater bottle*)

**Mrs Dawson**  Mother! Are you feeling better?
**Gran**  Not much. My hotwater bottle's cold.
**Mrs Dawson**  Give it to me. Mother — this is Bill West. This is my mother, Mrs Finlay, Bill.
**Gran**  How do you do?
**Bill**  Nice to meet you.
**Mrs Dawson**  You and Bill can have a chat, mother, while I go and fill this bottle.
**Gran**  All right.

(**Mrs Dawson** *goes out*)

**Bill**  I'm sorry you've been ill. Have you seen the doctor?
**Gran**  No. I've not much faith in doctors.
**Bill**  Oh.
**Gran**  I thought you'd be a younger man.
**Bill**  I sometimes wish I was.
**Gran**  You and Jane are thinking of getting married, are you?
**Bill**  It has been mentioned.
**Gran**  Have you been married before?
**Bill**  Yes. My wife died about six years ago.

**Gran**  I'm sorry. Do you have any children?
**Bill**  No.
**Gran**  Children can be a handful at times, specially if you've no experience of them. How do you think you're going to get along with Jane's two?
**Bill**  I just hope it will work out. I don't expect them to think of me as their real father.
**Gran**  You'd better not be like him. He walked out and left Jane flat when they were young. A real fly-by-night. I never liked him. Jill — the girl — won't have anything to do with him now.
**Bill**  Well, I hope it hasn't put her off the idea of fathers altogether. I know there'll be problems.
**Gran**  You'll be very set in your ways now, I should think. It's going to be very hard for you to make changes at your time of life.
**Bill**  Oh, I'm not all that old. We'll have to try to make it work. I'm very fond of Jane and I think she feels the same way about me. We've both been lonely.
**Gran**  Don't talk to me about being lonely. I lost my husband eight years ago.
**Bill**  I'm sorry. It's a bit hard to get over a loss like that, isn't it?
**Gran**  I've never been much of a one for making friends. And you can't make new friends when you're my age.
**Bill**  But you do have Jane and the children. Even if we get married, you'll still have them.
**Gran**  Will I?

(**Mrs Dawson** *comes back*)

**Mrs Dawson**  I've put your hotwater bottle back in your bed. You can go up again, if you like.
**Gran**  I'll stay here a bit.
**Mrs Dawson**  Was that the back door?
**Bill**  It sounded like someone coming in.
**Mrs Dawson**  I'll just have a look.

(**Mrs Dawson** *opens the door of the room and looks out*)

**Mrs Dawson**  Keith! Just where have you been? Come in here.

(**Keith** *comes in. He is very muddy*)

**Gran**   Just look at him! What on earth have you been doing? Your head's bleeding.
**Keith**   I came off that rotten bike.
**Gran**   You look as if you've been rolling in mud.
**Mrs Dawson**   Have you hurt yourself?
**Keith**   What does it look like? Of course I have. I've cut my head and banged my elbow and my knee.
**Mrs Dawson**   You're not old enough to be riding motor-bikes. Haven't you any sense?
**Keith**   There was something wrong with the bike, I tell you! It wasn't my fault. Don't be so stupid.
**Bill**   And it wasn't your mother's fault, either. There's no need to lose your temper with her.
**Keith**   What's it got to do with you?
**Mrs Dawson**   Don't be so cheeky. Go upstairs. Get those filthy clothes off and have a wash. I'll be up in a minute to see you.
**Keith**   Don't bother. I can look after myself.
**Mrs Dawson**   It doesn't look like it.

(**Keith** *goes out*)

**Gran**   He won't do that again in a hurry.
**Mrs Dawson**   I hope he hasn't really hurt himself.
**Bill**   I shouldn't think so, Jane. Just cuts and bruises. These things happen.
**Mrs Dawson**   I'm sorry he was rude, Bill. He isn't usually like that.
**Bill**   He probably felt a bit of a fool. Some people do lash out when they feel like that.
**Mrs Dawson**   He's been a bit of a handful lately.

(**Jill** *comes in, followed by* **Greg**)

**Greg**   Evening, Mrs Dawson. Evening, Mrs Finlay.
**Gran**   Hello.
**Mrs Dawson**   Hello, Greg.
**Jill**   You must be Mr West. I've heard a lot about you.
**Bill**   How do you do?

**Jill** I felt a bit mean having to dash out when you were coming.
**Bill** That's all right.
**Jill** We had to come back, anyway. Greg — we needed some money. This is Greg — Greg Southern.
**Greg** Hello.
**Bill** Funny. I seem to know your face.
**Greg** I don't think so.
**Bill** Don't you come from Moortown?
**Greg** Moortown?
**Bill** You wouldn't know a pub called the *Five Bells* there?
**Greg** Afraid I've never heard of it.
**Bill** I must be mistaken.
**Greg** Yes.
**Jill** Did you meet our Keith?
**Bill** Yes. Just. He came in a bit the worse for wear.
**Jill** Why? What happened?
**Greg** Look, Jill, I've just remembered. I promised to meet a bloke. We can't stop.
**Jill** You didn't say.
**Greg** I told you. I've just remembered.
**Mrs Dawson** You've got to go out again?
**Greg** Yes. We're late now. Jill — the money.
**Jill** Oh, yes. It was in a brown envelope, Mum.
**Mrs Dawson** It's in that end drawer over there.
**Jill** Here? (*She opens the drawer*) Oh, yes. I've got it.
**Greg** We've got to rush. That bloke will be waiting.
**Jill** All right.
**Greg** Sorry about that, Mrs Dawson. Goodnight, Mr — er —
**Bill** Goodnight.
**Mrs Dawson** Don't be late, Jill.
**Jill** No, Mum.

(**Jill** *and* **Greg** *go out*)

**Gran** Well! Talk about manners! Rush in, rush out. It's downright rude.
**Mrs Dawson** You did know him, Bill, didn't you?
**Bill** I can't really say.
**Mrs Dawson** And then you remembered something else

about him. I could see it in your face.
**Bill** No. I'm probably quite wrong.
**Mrs Dawson** Tell me.
**Bill** It wouldn't be fair. I may be mixing him up with someone else. How long has Jill been going out with him?
**Mrs Dawson** Three or four months on and off. Sometimes more off than on. Why ask? You do know something about him, don't you? Something bad?
**Bill** I'm not at all sure. And I'm not going to say anything until I am sure. I'll make a few enquiries.
**Mrs Dawson** If it affects Jill, I want to know.
**Bill** If I find it has got nothing to do with Greg, you'll have worried and I'll have stirred up pointless mischief. As soon as I know either way, I'll tell you. I promise.
**Mrs Dawson** I'm worried now.
**Bill** I'm sorry. Try and forget I spoke. Look — time's getting on and I mustn't miss that train. Let's have a cup of tea before I go.
**Mrs Dawson** All right. But I'd better go up and see to Keith first. Unless — Gran? Would you like to make us a cup of tea?
**Gran** Oh, I don't think I could. I'd better just sit quietly here.
**Bill** I'll make the tea.
**Mrs Dawson** You don't know where the things are.
**Bill** I can find them. I'm used to looking after things like that. You go on up to Keith.

(**Bill** *and* **Mrs Dawson** *leave the room*)


## Scene 3

(*The same room, later. It is empty except for* **Mrs Dawson**. **Jill** *comes in*)

**Jill** I thought you'd be in bed.
**Mrs Dawson** I've been thinking.
**Jill** Oh? Well – I'm going to bed.
**Mrs Dawson** You just don't care, do you?
**Jill** What are you talking about?

**Mrs Dawson**  I was ashamed tonight. I ask Bill here and you all run away from him.
**Jill**  We didn't run away.
**Mrs Dawson**  Gran says she's ill and doesn't want him to come. You go out to avoid him and Keith slips away and then comes in looking like a traffic accident. What sort of a family will he think he's getting?
**Jill**  He's not marrying any of us.
**Mrs Dawson**  He'd be your stepfather. Right from the start you show that you don't want to know him. What must he feel?
**Jill**  He'll get over it.
**Mrs Dawson**  After tonight he might not want to get married again at all.
**Jill**  That's his business. And you might be better off that way.
**Mrs Dawson**  You think so? Well — I suppose you're no worse than the other two. None of you has much understanding. Keith? He's too young. Gran doesn't try. She's too wrapped up in herself. So are you. None of you really cares about how I feel. Bill does.
**Jill**  That's not fair. I help you in the house. So does Keith sometimes.
**Mrs Dawson**  I'm not talking about that. Bill sees my point of view. He appreciates me. We share things. I can discuss things with him, get advice. I can't get any of that from you.
**Jill**  You're just tired. So am I. I'm going to bed.
**Mrs Dawson**  Not just yet. That money you came back for. It was for Greg, wasn't it?
**Jill**  What if it was? It's my money. I earned it.
**Mrs Dawson**  He's a sponger.
**Jill**  What do you know about it?
**Mrs Dawson**  I know he's a bad lot. What did he do in Moortown?
**Jill**  Moortown? So that's it, is it? Dear Bill has been spreading rumours. Greg said he would. What a slimy thing to do.
**Mrs Dawson**  You've no right to say that.
**Jill**  And you've no right to say things about Greg. You've been listening to lies.

**Mrs Dawson**   Bill said nothing about Greg. He didn't want to worry me. I told you — he cares about how I feel.
**Jill**   Cares? He's like an evil old woman with his gossip.
**Mrs Dawson**   You're talking about a man who could be your stepfather.
**Jill**   No, I'm not. He's a troublemaker. If he comes into this house, I'm leaving.
**Mrs Dawson**   Where could you go?
**Jill**   Don't you worry about that. I could go to Greg. We might even get married when his divorce comes through.
**Mrs Dawson**   Go, then! I know what it's like to be married to someone like Greg. You'll find out. I don't care any more.
**Jill**   I mean it.
**Mrs Dawson**   So do I. I've looked after this family for years. I've put you all first for too long. From tonight I'm going to consider myself, too. If Bill asks me to marry him, I will.
**Gran**   (*her voice comes faintly from upstairs*) Jane!
**Mrs Dawson**   Do you see what I mean? She's awake. She'll want to talk to me. She'll expect me to get her a drink.
**Gran**   (*from upstairs*) Jane!
**Mrs Dawson**   Tonight I'll attend to her. Afterwards — I've decided I'm going to have some life of my own. And that means sharing it with Bill, whatever you all say or do. So you can choose, too. You can stay or go.

(**Mrs Dawson** *goes out.* **Jill** *stands staring after her. Then she moves towards the door*)

**Jill**   Mum! Wait!

(**Jill** *goes out*)

---

## People in the play

1   Mrs Dawson gives her reasons for having asked Mr West to the house. Explain in your own words what these are.
2   Is Gran really ill? Or is she putting it on a bit to get attention? What do you think?
3   What was the first name of Mrs Dawson's husband? How

did he treat his family? What kind of a person does he seem to have been?
4 Do you think Jill gets on well with her grandmother or not? Give some evidence from the play to explain why you think as you do.
5 What do you think about Jill's attitude to her mother?
6 Is Bill West a man who takes offence easily or not? Why do you think so?
7 How well does he understand other people's points of view? Give some evidence from the play to show why you think as you do.
8 When she is alone with Bill West, Gran brings up the difficulties he will face if he marries her daughter. Explain what these difficulties might be. Why do you think she talks about them? Is she thinking of Bill or is there another reason?
9 What do you think of Mrs Dawson's accusation that the family 'ran away' from meeting Bill West? Is she right to be annoyed or is she overdoing it? Say why you think as you do.
10 Is Mrs Dawson being fair when she tells Jill that she can 'stay or go'? Do you agree with her? Explain why you judge her as you do.
11 How serious do you think Jill is about leaving?

## Families

1 Gran says that Mrs Dawson has been 'too soft' with her children. Do you think that Mrs Dawson should have been stricter with them both, or do you think her attitude to them is right?
2 Bill West tries not to worry Mrs Dawson with what he seems to have heard about Greg. Should he have told her? Is it sometimes necessary to repeat gossip or to tell tales about other people, or is it always wrong? What do you think?
3 Gran accuses Jill of being 'selfish'. How selfish is Gran herself? Is Mrs Dawson selfish to want the children to stay in and meet Mr West? Who do you think is the most selfish person in the play?

**Writing**

1 Why does Jill ask her mother to wait at the end of the play? Does it seem as if her mother has never spoken to her like that before? Does Jill want to apologise to Mrs Dawson? How does Mrs Dawson react? Has she calmed down? Or is she still angry? Write the scene in the form of a play.

2 Do you agree with Mrs Dawson that Keith seems 'a bit of a handful'? Or does his behaviour seem understandable for a boy in his teens? Give your opinion of the way Keith behaves.

3 Gran complains of being lonely. What do you think are the main problems of being old? Lack of money? Illness? Lack of friends? You could write your answer as if you really were an old person.

4 What is the truth about Greg? Is Bill West mistaken and mixing Greg up with someone else? If so, does he meet Jill and Greg and apologise? How do Greg and Jill react to that? Do they accept the apology or are they annoyed? Or has Greg done something wrong in Moortown? Has he cheated someone out of money? Has he been in trouble with the police? What kind of trouble? Does he admit it? Does it make any difference to Jill's feelings about him? Write the scene in the form of a play.

# You, the Jury

---

Mr Crompton  
Miss Ellerby  
Miss Marley  } *the finalists*  
Mr Silkin  
Mr Miller  
Mrs Wise  
**Mr Weinberger,** *a millionaire*  
**Clerk**  
**Jury leader**  
**The jury** (*the rest of the class*)

---

## Scene 1

(*A room in the town hall at Duxford*)

**Clerk** Good morning. You are the six finalists picked out by Mr Weinberger. May I wish you all well in presenting your worthy cases. This could take a long time, though Mr Weinberger does want a decision today. You, the jury, please listen attentively to all that is said by the finalists. Perhaps you would all stand when Mr Weinberger comes in. Ah, here he comes, precisely on time.

(**Mr Weinberger** *enters. They all stand*)

**Clerk** Good morning, Mr Weinberger.  
**Mr Weinberger** Good morning. Can we begin right away?  
**Clerk** Would you like to open the meeting with a few words?  
**Mr Weinberger** It will be a few. I'll get quickly to the point. As you all know I was born in this city. I love it. I made my first pound here. It means a great deal to me. In honour of

my son, who was so tragically killed last month, I have decided to give a sum of money to the city.

**Clerk** If we could offer our sympathy and condolences——

**Mr Weinberger** Thank you. I have, therefore, decided to give twenty million pounds to the most worthy cause.

**Clerk** Twenty million! I thought it was ten million.

**Mr Weinberger** My wife and I discussed it again last night. We wish to double it.

**Clerk** It is the most generous offer I have ever heard of.

**Mr Weinberger** I want a really fitting memorial to my son. Can we begin at once, please?

**Clerk** You six finalists know the rules, though you may have to adjust your case because of the increased offer. Each of you will have one chance only to state your reasons for receiving the twenty million. After you have all spoken the jury alone will decide which cause is the most deserving. Mr Weinberger may question you but he will not vote in the final decision. You have all drawn lots for speaking order. Mr Crompton, please begin.

**Mr Crompton** I represent the town council. I would like to thank Mr Weinberger for his most generous offer. I must bore you first with a little history — essential history, though.

**Mr Weinberger** Don't be too long.

**Mr Crompton** I won't. This city was nothing but a village before the Industrial Revolution. Then came the machines, and the cotton that made this city great. The main part of the city was built in Victorian times. You can see this in a walk round the city square. It still looks a grand town.

**Clerk** We all know that. Please get on with your argument.

**Mr Crompton** I am coming to the main point. Mr Weinberger says that he loves this city. I wonder if he would love what is behind the face of the city square: rotting roofs, crumbling plaster, woodworm. Our national heritage — the town centre — is in danger of falling down. And now that another ten million has been added we could have new amenities — a theatre and concert hall, with an art gallery. We could also have a public garden with a piece of sculpture in remembrance of Mr Weinberger's son. We would call it the Weinberger Centre.

**Mr Weinberger**   Cannot the Government and the Arts Council help?

**Mr Crompton**   The Government says it is the town's problem and the Arts Council will pay only part.

**Mr Weinberger**   Why not raise the rates?

**Mr Crompton**   I have left the most important part to last. Underneath the town centre the sewers are crumbling. Only last month, as you know, a hole the size of a double-decker bus appeared in the square. We will have to put the rates up considerably to repair the sewers. We cannot have a new centre as well. If the sewers are not rebuilt there could be a serious outbreak of disease — perhaps cholera. It makes sense to do both schemes together.

**Clerk**   I think you have made your point.

**Mr Crompton**   I do not think any of the rest of you can have a better case than this.

**Clerk**   We shall see. Miss Ellerby, please.

**Miss Ellerby**   You all know that for a town of our size the hospital accommodation is a disgrace. I represent the hospital board. There is not enough accommodation and what there is is falling down. Some patients are in huts put up as a temporary measure in the last war. A surgeon told me this week that he had to stop a delicate eye operation because of rain falling through the roof. I also feel sorry for the children. A girl having her tonsils out could be in a bed next to an old lady dying of cancer. It's a disgrace.

**Mr Weinberger**   What about the National Health Service? Can't they rebuild?

**Miss Ellerby**   We are not at the top of the list. We may have to wait five years.

**Mr Crompton**   You will have even more serious cases if the sewers are not repaired.

**Clerk**   Please, Mr Crompton, you have had your say.

**Mr Weinberger**   Would my son have been saved if you had had more life-support machinery?

**Miss Ellerby**   He would have stood a better chance. We want to do more research on the care of people injured in road accidents. The extra ten million would provide a research unit. We would call it the Weinberger Accident Research Unit.

**Mr Weinberger** Thank you.

**Clerk** Miss Marley, please.

**Miss Marley** You all know about the unemployment situation. You have seen the young people hanging around the streets of Duxford with nothing to do. Cotton no longer makes this town prosperous, so why do we need a grand town centre? I think the money should be spent on youth by providing leisure and sporting facilities throughout the city. We could build several free leisure and sporting centres and buy a supply of equipment to last for years. We could have swimming pools and ice rinks. The extra ten million could provide training centres for the unemployed. We must not make our schoolchildren or our youngsters feel useless. Many people now in employment could be put out of work by computers, so the problem will grow. Miss Ellerby mentioned physical illness. What about mental illness caused by having nothing to do and feeling useless?

**Clerk** Have you finished?

**Miss Marley** There's much more I could say.

**Mr Weinberger** I had very little as a boy. Don't you think children of today are spoiled?

**Miss Marley** Don't blame the youth of today for the age they live in. Come with me into the cafés and listen to them as they try to pass the time. I don't find them spoiled.

**Mr Weinberger** Thank you.

**Clerk** Mr Silkin, please.

**Mr Silkin** I think we must look a little wider than Duxford. The country desperately needs modern factories that can export. I have invented a new lightweight material for space research. Here on earth it could replace asbestos. It needs developing fast before the Japanese do it. I need money to build a factory and set up production lines. Twenty million would provide five hundred jobs, perhaps even more. We would not need all the things Miss Marley asks for if the young people were usefully employed. And the town would be richer and able to pay for better medical treatment. Perhaps we could even make enough money to help the council with the sewers.

**Mr Crompton** I doubt it. I have heard of these fancy space schemes before. Most of them go bankrupt. My scheme would give the town a new heart and employ three hundred men.

**Clerk** Please, you have had your say.

**Mr Silkin** Men, you say. What about women? I would employ women as well.

**Mr Weinberger** What is your business experience, Mr Silkin?

**Mr Silkin** I have worked for ten years in industry as a manager. I know a good thing when I see it. The export potential is tremendous.

**Mr Weinberger** You expect to make a large profit?

**Mr Silkin** The factory could be a co-operative. The workers could share in the profits and therefore the town would, too. It would be called the Weinberger Space Research Co-operative.

**Clerk** Thank you. Mr Miller, please.

**Mr Miller** All these plans seem deserving. But before anything else people must live somewhere. I'll be frank: the council made a mistake in the building of the Fore Street high-rise flats. The concrete is crumbling. The flats are damp and cost too much to heat. We want to pull them down at a cost of four million. Then we could use the rest of the money to erect new two-storey dwellings with small gardens. They would be for the whole community, but particularly the old and the newly wed. We would call it Weinberger Way.

**Mr Weinberger** What about the Government?

**Mr Miller** They say it must come from the rates. We can't go on putting up the rates.

**Mr Weinberger** Is there any guarantee you won't make another mistake?

**Mr Miller** We have learnt our lesson as far as housing is concerned.

**Mr Weinberger** Thank you.

**Clerk** Mrs Wise, please.

**Mrs Wise**   I have listened to all the others and I must say that they have good cases. But, by and large, the people of this country are well housed, well fed and have good medical and sporting facilities. I have been to many eastern countries where millions have no proper water supply. This causes dreadful disease and early death. If only you had seen the thin, wasting children. If only you had heard their cries and screams. If only you had seen the blindness and the look of hopelessness. I propose, Mr Weinberger, that we set up an organisation to fight this problem, with its headquarters here in Duxford. It would be called the Weinberger Water for the World Project.

**Mr Weinberger**   Do you not believe that charity begins at home?

**Mrs Wise**   Charity does not. Charity begins where the human need is greatest. I can never forget what I have seen. Try drinking filthy muddy water for a week.

**Mr Weinberger**   Thank you.

**Clerk**   Have you finished?

**Mrs Wise**   I would like to show my slides.

**Clerk**   No, we have not allowed the others to show slides or film.

**Mrs Wise**   But you should see them.

**Clerk**   No. You have all had your time. Well, members of the jury, you have heard of six deserving causes. Which one should have the money? Mr Weinberger, do you want a further word?

**Mr Weinberger**   I do not want to influence the jury in any way.

**Jury leader**   The jury would like to ask if it is possible to divide the money.

**Mr Weinberger**   No, it is not. A condition of my giving this money is that the most deserving cause gets it all.

**Clerk**   Jury, you must make your decision.

*(Here the class discusses and votes)*

## People in the play

1. Which person do you think presents his or her case best?
2. Is Mr Weinberger fair with all the candidates?
3. What kind of a man do you imagine him to be?
4. Why might he leave it to a jury to decide?
5. What kind of person might Mr Crompton be?
6. Are the women as forceful as the men in their arguments?
7. Should Mrs Wise have been allowed to show her slides?
8. How does the clerk conduct the meeting? Could it have been more friendly?
9. Which finalists want your sympathy for sick people? Does this make their cases stronger?
10. Have any of the finalists anything personal to gain from winning?

## A gift of money

1. Whichever way the class voted, what was your own view?
2. How do you feel the older people of Duxford would have voted?
3. Can we afford to send large sums of money abroad for charity?
4. Should the rates pay for all the amenities in a town?
5. Is it wrong that Mr Weinberger had £20 million to give in the first place? Explain your answer.

## Writing

1. Write down what the winner said to the meeting.
2. In play form, write what Mr Weinberger said to his wife after the meeting.
3. Explain what you would do if you received £50,000 and you could not spend it on yourself or your family.
4. Write the newspaper report about the winning cause that appears in the *Duxford Echo*, complete with headline.
5. Find out what the Arts Council does. Then in a few sentences say if you think it should spend money in your area.

# Home Sweet Home

Simon  ⎫
Keith  ⎟ *four squatters*
Andrea ⎟
Louise ⎭

Gareth ⎫ *nationalist extremists*
Meg    ⎭

Mr Barker  ⎫ *a retired couple*
Mrs Barker ⎭

Policeman
Policewoman

## Scene 1

(*Outside an old cottage in North Wales.* **Simon, Keith, Andrea** *and* **Louise** *are trying to get in.*)

**Simon**  Try that window.
**Keith**  I think I can open this one.
**Simon**  The other looks easier. There's a bit of a gap.
**Keith**  Right.
**Andrea**  Do you think we should? Isn't it burglary?
**Simon**  No.
**Andrea**  Well, breaking and entering?
**Keith**  I think it's just trespass. They can't do you for that. We don't really know if anyone owns it. Some of these old cottages don't really belong to anyone.
**Andrea**  They must do.
**Louise**  You go ahead and quickly. It's beginning to rain. I don't want another night with a baby in a leaking caravan.

**Andrea**  This place may leak more than the caravan.
**Louise**  At least we can repair it. The caravan was beyond repair.
**Simon**  It looks pretty good from the outside. It can't be worse than the caravan.
**Keith**  What luck! The catch is off. I'll climb in and see if I can open the door.
**Simon**  I'll keep watch. Try the back door, if the front door won't open.


## Scene 2

(*Inside the cottage*)

**Louise**  We're in luck. It's dry.
**Andrea**  It's in a very bad condition though.
**Simon**  What do you expect, love, the Ritz?
**Louise**  My baby will be much better here.
**Andrea**  What happens when someone tells the police?
**Keith**  We stay put. Squatters' rights. I think three of us should always be in the house.
**Andrea**  That'll be awkward. We'll need to shop. You'll have to look for work.
**Keith**  We'll manage.
**Simon**  We may be lucky. I've had my eye on this place. It's been empty for two years since that old woman died. No one seems to want it. There has been no 'For Sale' notice.
**Louise**  If we don't occupy it, you know what will happen. It will become a second home for some rich person from the Midlands. Do check if the water's on, Keith.
**Keith**  O.K.
**Simon**  There's no electricity.
**Louise**  We can manage with paraffin. Go out to the van for some, Simon. I want to warm the baby's bottle.
**Simon**  Right, I'll start bringing our stuff in. It's getting dark.
**Andrea**  There's a lovely view from upstairs.
**Louise**  I wouldn't care if you could see the gasworks. It's home sweet home for the first time in two years.

## Scene 3

(*A week later.* **Keith** *and* **Louise** *are upstairs*)

**Louise**  There, the baby is quiet now. We can get some sleep.
**Keith**  I certainly need it. I've worked hard on that kitchen today.
**Louise**  You have, love. Just a minute.
**Keith**  What is it?
**Louise**  I heard a noise downstairs.
**Keith**  You're always hearing noises.
**Louise**  No, there *is* something.
**Keith**  Is it the police?
**Louise**  This is what I've been dreading.

(**Andrea** *rushes in*)

**Andrea**  There's someone downstairs.
**Keith**  I'll get Simon.
**Andrea**  He's coming.
**Louise**  I'll get the baby.


## Scene 4

(*Downstairs. It is dark*)

**Simon**  Who is it? Shine the torch on them, Keith.
**Keith**  The catch is stuck.
**Gareth**  Who the hell are you?
**Simon**  More to the point, who are you?
**Meg**  Are you the new owner?
**Simon**  We're living here.
**Gareth**  You own it?
**Simon**  We claim squatters' rights.
**Keith**  Got it! They're masked! They've got petrol cans! They've come to burn us out! Stop them!
**Gareth**  Just a minute! Just a minute! If you're squatters, it could alter the case. We heard that this place had been sold as a second home. The group we belong to believes in homes for people in their own homeland. We think local

people should have the first chance of housing.
**Meg**  Do you come from this area?
**Simon**  I was born here. So was my wife.
**Meg**  That does alter the case.
**Louise**  (*coming down holding the baby*) What is it?
**Keith**  It's some friends. It's all right.
**Louise**  Thank goodness for that. Andrea's afraid to come down.
**Gareth**  How many are there of you?
**Louise**  Four and my baby.
**Meg**  You must stay here then.
**Gareth**  Yes, stay here. But don't tell anyone we've been here. You haven't seen us.
**Meg**  Good luck to you.
**Gareth**  Here's a phone number to ring if you are thrown out.

(**Gareth** *and* **Meg** *go*)

**Louise**  Thank goodness the baby kept us awake. We could have been burnt in our beds.
**Simon**  I've heard of that group before. I'd like to join them.
**Keith**  Probably better not to. Arson is a serious crime.
**Andrea**  (*coming down*) Is everything all right? What was it?
**Simon**  Come back upstairs. I'll tell you all about it.

## Scene 5

(*A week later.* **Louise** *and* **Andrea** *are downstairs*)

**Louise**  I do hope the baby sleeps. He was very sick.
**Andrea**  I'm sure he will. Well, we've been here a fortnight.
**Louise**  It's like heaven. I'm going to start work on the garden tomorrow. Just think, if we stay here, the baby can play in the garden.
**Andrea**  When he's bigger we can make a swing on the apple tree.
**Louise**  What a lovely idea.

(*A car draws up outside*)

**Andrea**  Oh no, a car!

**Louise**  Let me see.
**Andrea**  I told Simon and Keith not to go out together. There should always be three of us. They've got too confident.
**Louise**  They should be back soon. They couldn't miss the chance of a day's work.
**Andrea**  It's a man and a woman. They're quite old.
**Louise**  They're coming in.
**Andrea**  I'll put a chair under the door handle.
**Louise**  I'll do the same at the back.
**Andrea**  Hurry!

(*They do this*)

**Mr Barker**  (*voice off*) I can't open the door.
**Mrs Barker**  (*voice off*) Have you got the right key?
**Mr Barker**  Of course I've got the right key.
**Mrs Barker**  Well, push. It's probably damp making it stick.
**Mr Barker**  No, it seems jammed.
**Mrs Barker**  We'll try the back door.
**Mr Barker**  Right.

(*The baby cries out*)

**Mrs Barker**  Did you hear that?
**Mr Barker**  What?
**Mrs Barker**  It sounded like a baby. I think there's someone living here.
**Louise**  (*whispering*) Oh no, the baby.
**Mrs Barker**  There is a baby crying in there. There's a table and things. I can see them.
**Mr Barker**  Let's get the police. Come on.
**Andrea**  Oh, I do hope Simon and Keith get back soon.

## Scene 6

(*The same, a quarter of an hour later.* **Simon** *and* **Keith** *return*)

**Andrea**  Quick, Simon, come in. People have been here. They must own it.
**Simon**  Right, Keith, nail those planks we got ready to the

door frames. They'll have to have a battering ram to get us out of here.
**Keith**   O.K.
**Andrea**   Quick! The police are coming!
**Simon**   I'll talk to them from upstairs. Keep them guessing while Keith nails up the doors.

(*Sound of hammering*)

## Scene 7

(*Upstairs, ten minutes later.* **Simon** *and* **Keith** *are standing near an open window*)

**Policeman**   (*voice off*) Will whoever is in there come out and talk to me, please?
**Keith**   Take no notice.
**Policeman**   Will you please come out, all of you?
**Simon**   What do you want?
**Policeman**   I have a man here who claims to be the owner of this cottage. Will you tell me what right you have in there, sir?
**Simon**   Squatters' rights.
**Mrs Barker**   (*voice off*) This is our home. It's our retirement home.
**Simon**   We're not budging.
**Policeman**   It would be best if you all came out quietly.
**Mr Barker**   You've no right to be there.
**Simon**   I expect it's a second home for you. We've got no home.
**Mr Barker**   It's not. We're selling our house in the town to buy this one. We're going to retire here.
**Mrs Barker**   We're going to do this place up.
**Simon**   So you can afford two houses. We can't afford one.
**Policewoman**   (*voice off*) It would help if you stopped shouting and came down here.

(**Andrea** *comes in*)

**Andrea**   Where are we going to live? You tell me that.
**Policewoman**   Where did you come from?

**Andrea** You try two years in a leaking caravan.
**Policeman** I can get other officers.
**Andrea** Bullies. What a country!

(**Louise** *comes in*)

**Louise** We have a sick baby in here.
**Mrs Barker** What a way to treat pensioners. I shall faint. I know I will.
**Mr Barker** There, dear. We've worked all our lives for a house in the country.
**Simon** We've worked too, when we've been able to find work, but we've got nothing.
**Andrea** You give us a decent home.
**Louise** Then we'll come out all right, but not before.
**Keith** Yes, go and fetch someone on the Council.
**Mrs Barker** Are they gypsies?
**Policewoman** I don't think so.

# Scene 8

(*Downstairs, the next day*)

**Policeman** (*voice off*) I'll give you one last chance to come out. I have an order to get you out.
**Simon** Stand by the door, Keith.
**Louise** The baby's ill and in pain. It could be appendicitis. We'll have to take him to hospital.
**Simon** As soon as we open that door, they're in.
**Louise** We've got no choice. He's been awake all night.
**Policewoman** (*voice off*) Let us in, please.
**Keith** Give him some more medicine.
**Louise** It's no good, Keith.
**Andrea** We must think of the baby.
**Simon** Well, it was nice while it lasted. Take off the planks, Keith.

(**Keith** *starts to do this*)

**Louise** We'll never have that swing you dreamt of.
**Andrea** No picnics under the apple tree.

**Louise**  Goodbye garden.
**Andrea**  Goodbye house.

(*The four squatters leave the house*)

## Scene 9

(*The same, some minutes later.* **Mr and Mrs Barker** *enter cautiously*)

**Mrs Barker**  Have they done any damage?
**Mr Barker**  I'll have to have a good look.
**Mrs Barker**  What a state it's in. I'm sure they're gypsies. Can we sue them?
**Mr Barker**  I'll have to look into it.
**Mrs Barker**  What a way to treat pensioners.
**Mr Barker**  I don't know what this country's coming to. To think that I fought in the war so people could have a decent life.
**Mrs Barker**  Some people seem to think they can have things for nothing. Forty years I worked in that biscuit factory.
**Mr Barker**  Let's get the camping stove going and have a cup of tea.
**Mrs Barker**  I thought the country would suit my nerves better. What a start. I'm all of a tremble.
**Mr Barker**  I'll make you a nice cup of tea, love.

---

## People in the play

1  Who is the least sure about breaking into the cottage?
2  Who is the most determined to break in, Simon or Keith? Or are they equally determined?
3  What kind of mother is Louise?
4  Who is the most frightened when Gareth and Meg break in?
5  How would you describe the four people who break in? What sort of people are they?
6  Does the baby make any difference to their right to be there or not? Why do you think that?

7   What kind of person is Mrs Barker?
8   Do the policeman and policewoman do their duty properly?
9   Who expects most from the cottage?
10  What sort of person is Gareth?

## Squatting

1  Has everyone the right to a decent home? Or must everyone expect to work hard for it? What are your views?
2  Why might these four not have repaired the caravan?
3  Whom are you in sympathy with in this play? Do you feel sympathy for more than one character?
4  Should people with babies have priority for council accommodation? If so, would this be fair to old people and newly weds?
5  If you have the money should you be able to buy more than one house? What are your views?
6  Is it right to use force to achieve something you think is important?
7  Do you think it is right to keep houses for the people who live in an area?

## Writing

1  Write a newspaper report on the break-in and eviction. You can invent surnames.
2  Write the conversation, as a play, when the squatters return to collect their few bits of furniture from the front garden.
3  Write your views about the need for better housing in a letter to a newspaper.
4  Write a letter from Mrs Barker to a friend telling her about what happened.
5  Draw a plan of an old cottage both downstairs and upstairs. You could draw a further plan of how you would improve it.
6  Write the story of what happened to the four and the baby after they left the cottage.

# Neighbours

Mr Smith
Mrs Smith
Mr Jones
Mrs Jones
Julie Smith
Andrew Jones

## Scene 1

(*Flat 101 on the fourteenth floor of a tower block of flats*)

**Mr Smith**   Oh, damn!
**Mrs Smith**   (*voice off*) What is it?
**Mr Smith**   The television.
**Mrs Smith**   (*coming in from the kitchen*) Has the picture gone wrong again?
**Mr Smith**   Yes, look at all those lines.
**Mrs Smith**   Let me try.
**Mr Smith**   It's no good. I bet it's him next door again using his power drill. I'm sure I can hear it.
**Mrs Smith**   You asked him to fit a suppressor.
**Mr Smith**   Do you think a man like that would bother? Not him. No, not him.
**Mrs Smith**   I didn't want to tell you but a bottle of milk was missing again this morning.
**Mr Smith**   Their damn kids. I think we should go to the police.
**Mrs Smith**   I knew it would make you mad. Mrs Ellis saw the milkman leave it and their kids playing around with it.

**Mr Smith**  And the lift wasn't working again this evening. I had to walk up fourteen flights.

**Mrs Smith**  You've told me twice.

**Mr Smith**  I'm sure it's their kids. They keep pressing the buttons and jamming the doors.

**Mrs Smith**  They run up and down the stairs as well. Nearly knocked me down. And the things they write on the walls! I think we should write to the Council and get them moved.

**Mr Smith**  Look at that picture. I'm going to have it out with him.

**Mrs Smith**  It's not just him, it's her as well. I'm sure she deliberately bangs her vacuum cleaner against the wall while she's cleaning. I can never have a lie down in the afternoon. There! She's just slammed that door again. That's how it is all day. It gets on my nerves.

**Mr Smith**  Just wait till the morning. I'll see him. It's better now. He must have stopped.

**Mrs Smith**  Julie's not in yet.

**Mr Smith**  She gets later and later. Where is she?

**Mrs Smith**  At her friend Anne's, I think. Turn it up a bit, will you?

## Scene 2

*(Flat 102 next door)*

**Mr Jones**  I've finished. That's a good job done.

**Mrs Jones**  I'll make you a cup of tea. Oh, no! They've turned up their television set again. It really is too bad. I wanted an early night. The children are sickening for something.

**Mr Jones**  I'll knock on the wall.

**Mrs Jones**  No, don't do that.

**Mr Jones**  Well, I'll go round and see him then.

**Mrs Jones**  Leave it till the morning. I can't stand a row tonight. I've got a headache.

**Mr Jones**  They really are thick, aren't they? I didn't tell you what I found when I got home tonight.

**Mrs Jones**  What?

**Mr Jones** Dog mess. Right by the door.
**Mrs Jones** That's their dog again. I hate cleaning it up.
**Mr Jones** Fancy keeping a dog fourteen storeys up.
**Mrs Jones** Poor thing. I don't blame the dog.
**Mr Jones** I think I'll write to the Council about it.
**Mrs Jones** It could give the kids eye disease. They play so much on that landing. And she pretends to be so high and mighty.
**Mr Jones** I'll go round.
**Mrs Jones** Not now. In the morning. Let's try and get some sleep in case the children wake up.
**Mr Jones** If his damn television set will let us.
**Mrs Jones** And if that girl of theirs doesn't start playing her pop records.
**Mr Jones** Is Andrew in yet?
**Mrs Jones** No.
**Mr Jones** I know he's eighteen, but he won't be fit for work with the hours he keeps.
**Mrs Jones** Come on.

## Scene 3

(*The landing between Flat 101 and Flat 102 next morning*)

**Mr Smith** (*stopping* **Mr Jones**) Ah! I wanted a word with you. I thought I asked you to fit a suppressor to that power drill.
**Mr Jones** I have fitted one.
**Mr Smith** Well, you can't have fitted it properly. My telly was on the blink last night.
**Mr Jones** I don't believe that. I could hear every word through the wall. It took us ages to get to sleep.
**Mrs Jones** (*coming out*) That's right. You tell him.
**Mr Smith** It wasn't too loud. I had to turn it up because you were ruining the reception.
**Mrs Jones** Three hours' sleep, that's all I've had.
**Mrs Smith** (*coming out*) I'm not surprised. Your children woke me up, too. Can't you see to them when they cry?
**Mrs Jones** I can't help it if they're ill.
**Mrs Smith** I expect they've drunk too much milk.

**Mrs Jones**  Just what do you mean by that?
**Mrs Smith**  A bottle of milk has disappeared again.
**Mr Jones**  Are you accusing my kids?
**Mr Smith**  They were seen playing around nearby a few minutes before it disappeared.
**Mr Jones**  There are other children besides ours who play on this landing.
**Mrs Jones**  Yes, our children would never do a thing like that.
**Mrs Smith**  Wouldn't they just!
**Mr Jones**  Well, what about your dog then?
**Mr Smith**  What about it?
**Mr Jones**  It's messed by my door again.
**Mr Smith**  My dog wouldn't do a thing like that. It's house-trained.
**Mr Jones**  It's the only dog on the landing.
**Mrs Smith**  Other dogs come up here.
**Mr Jones**  Well, I'm going to write to the Council about it.
**Mr Smith**  And I'm going to ring the police about the milk.
**Mr Jones**  Right, you do that. You *will* look a fool.
**Mr Smith**  I'll show you who's a fool. You're the worst neighbours we've ever had.
**Mr Jones**  And I would pay not to live by you. You're a menace.
**Mr Smith**  I'll lay one on you.
**Mrs Smith**  No, come on in.
**Mr Jones**  Just you try it then. Insulting my children.
**Mrs Jones**  No, Phil.
**Mr Jones**  I'm not afraid of him.
**Mrs Jones**  Come in and write to the Council.

## Scene 4

(*Flat 101 a few minutes later*)

**Mr Smith**  You wouldn't think a police station would be always engaged, would you?
**Mrs Smith**  Dial 999.
**Mr Smith**  It's not an emergency.
**Mrs Smith**  It's theft and abuse.

(**Julie** *comes in*)

**Julie** Why are you ringing the police?
**Mr Smith** It's those damn Joneses again.
**Julie** I heard you having a row. I want to talk to you about it.
**Mr Smith** Something else they've done? What is it?
**Julie** It's about Andrew.
**Mr Smith** Andrew?
**Julie** Their son.
**Mrs Smith** What's he done?
**Julie** He's done nothing. I'm going out with him. It's serious.
**Mrs Smith** A family like that? You can't.
**Mr Smith** How long has this been going on?
**Julie** Six months. I've had a long time to think about it.
**Mrs Smith** So you weren't with Anne?
**Julie** No.
**Mrs Smith** You're only seventeen. You can't know your own mind.
**Julie** I've never been surer in my life.
**Mr Smith** I'm going to put a stop to this, my girl.
**Julie** If you do, I shall leave home and go and live with him.
**Mrs Smith** You wouldn't do anything so stupid at your age.
**Julie** I would.
**Mr Smith** Well, I'll be damned. After the careful way we've brought you up.
**Julie** I'm very serious. So don't phone, please.

# Scene 5

(*Flat 102*)

**Mrs Jones** You tell them straight. Don't leave anything out.
**Andrew** What's going on now?
**Mrs Jones** Your father's writing to the Council.
**Andrew** What about?
**Mr Jones** That Smith family.
**Mrs Jones** I'll have them out of there, if it's the last thing I do.
**Andrew** I want to talk to you about them.

**Mr Jones**  He hasn't scraped your car again, has he?
**Andrew**  No. I'm going out with Julie.
**Mrs Jones**  The daughter?
**Andrew**  Yes.
**Mrs Jones**  You can't be serious. A stuck-up family like that.
**Andrew**  Julie's not stuck-up. I love her very much.
**Mr Jones**  You must be mad.
**Andrew**  She's a wonderful girl. We're going to get engaged.
**Mrs Jones**  I couldn't possibly be connected with a family like that. Who'd have children! And I thought you were old enough to act sensibly. I thought all my trouble was with the twins.
**Mr Jones**  I forbid it.
**Andrew**  I'm eighteen. You can't stop me.
**Mrs Jones**  You've kept all this from me.
**Andrew**  We had to, didn't we?
**Mr Jones**  You young fool.
**Andrew**  We plan to get married next year.
**Mrs Jones**  How will you manage? You haven't finished your apprenticeship yet.
**Andrew**  Julie has a good wage.
**Mrs Jones**  She's not pregnant, is she?
**Andrew**  No, she's not pregnant! Look, we've talked this over. We know our own minds. We want you to talk over your quarrel sensibly. We don't want to think that our parents are at each others' throats all the time.
**Mr Jones**  You mean talk to *them*? You must be joking.
**Mrs Jones**  It's gone too far.
**Andrew**  And before it goes any further we want you to meet and talk. Julie has a friend called Anne. She's lent us her flat for the evening —
**Mrs Jones**  So that's where you've been going.
**Andrew**  Listen, will you? Julie is going to cook a meal there tonight for all of us. We want you to meet on neutral ground and talk over your problems sensibly.
**Mrs Jones**  I'm not going. Nor is your father.
**Andrew**  You are, Mum, or I'll leave home and you won't see me again.
**Mrs Jones**  What a thing to say to your mother!

**Andrew** It's got to be said.
**Mr Jones** You're really serious, then?
**Andrew** I am.

## Scene 6

*(Anne's flat that evening)*

**Mr Jones** Now we can have this out.
**Mr Smith** We certainly can.
**Andrew** We're not here to shout at each other or to quarrel. You four are going to talk sensibly. Now what are your complaints, Mr Smith? Let's hear them.
**Mr Smith** It's his power drill; it ruins my television reception. His kids pinch our milk. They write on our walls. Worst of all they damage the lifts.
**Julie** What proof have you got, Dad?
**Mr Smith** I don't need proof. I know.
**Andrew** Dad, let's hear your complaints.
**Mr Jones** He knows well enough. His telly keeps us awake. His dog's mucky. It messes by our door.
**Mr Smith** My dog's clean!
**Mr Jones** It's not!
**Andrew** So you're at war for a few petty things like that.
**Mrs Jones** That's not the half of it.
**Mr Smith** They're not petty. Not if you have to walk up fourteen storeys.
**Andrew** They would look petty written down. Shall I write them down?
**Mr Jones** Don't be stupid.
**Andrew** It's you four who are being stupid. There's got to be give and take.
**Julie** We'll tell you what we think. If anyone's to blame, it's the Council for putting us on top of an anthill. For putting us up in the sky with lifts that break down easily. For building flats with thin walls. For not building proper houses with gardens. But you've either got to adapt to life there or get out. Fighting your neighbours doesn't help one bit. Andrew and I can see it clearly. Why can't you?

**Mr Smith**  Yes, but ——
**Andrew**  But nothing. First of all we'd like you to try to stop irritating each other. Check the power drill. Turn down the telly. Speak to the kids. Make sure the dog goes out. Then go and talk to each other regularly to break down the tension those flats build up.
**Julie**  We also want you to join the Residents' Association to fight for better conditions and proper houses.
**Mr Smith**  I don't know what to say.
**Mrs Jones**  Neither do I.
**Mrs Smith**  We've no choice, have we? I don't want to lose a daughter.
**Mrs Jones**  And I don't want to lose a son.
**Mr Jones**  It's not going to be as easy as all that.
**Andrew**  Peace is not easy, is it? But you must try.
**Mr Jones**  Very well, as long as ——
**Julie**  Don't start making conditions. Trust each other to put things right.
**Mr Jones**  I'll do my best, then.
**Mr Smith**  Me too.
**Andrew**  Right. Now I think we can eat. Dad, you'll see what a wife I've got.
**Julie**  We're not married yet.
**Andrew**  You know what I mean.
**Julie**  What about the wine?
**Andrew**  Yes, we're going to drink to all our futures. I paid a lot for this, so you'd better not let me down!
**Mrs Jones**  We won't, son.
**Mr Smith**  We won't, either. Let's drink a toast. Here's to all of us.
**All**  To all of us.

———

## People in the play

1  Which family has more to complain about? List the complaints made by each family.
2  Who suffers most from nerves?

3  What evidence is there that the twins stole the milk and damaged the lift?
4  Who seems to be the most handy about the home?
5  What evidence is there that the Smiths' dog messed by the door? Should they keep a dog in a high-rise flat?
6  Who is the most aggressive in the quarrel on the landing?
7  Who makes the most insulting remarks in the quarrel?
8  In what ways are Andrew and Julie nicer and more sensible than their parents?
9  What is their chance of a happy marriage considering their family background?
10 What hope is there at the end of the play that the families will get on?

## Neighbours' quarrels

1  Why do you think the authors called the families Smith and Jones?
2  Whom would you blame for the quarrel? The families? The Council? The builders? Children?
3  Does this play show you at all why wars occur between nations?
4  Why might young people get on better together than older people?
5  How could a residents' association help to stop quarrels between neighbours?

## Writing

1  Make a list of things neighbours and children might quarrel about. Put a star beside those problems which are hardest to solve.
2  In play form write the conversation the morning after the meal in either the Smiths' or the Jones's flat.
3  Write an unrhymed poem or a story called 'Neighbours' Quarrels'.
4  Andrew and Julie plan to live away from the flats when they are married. Write the conversation they have about the kind of home they want.

# The Shelter

**Mum**
**Dad**
**Mandy** ⎫
**Linda** ⎬ *their children*
**Tony** ⎭
**Uncle Wilf**
**Aunty Kate**, *Mum's sister*
**Mrs Benson**, *an elderly neighbour*
**Jim Hebden**, *a man lodging with Mrs Benson*

(*The scene is a nuclear shelter. It is lit by electricity and there is a door at one end. It is furnished with bunk beds and the characters are sitting on these.*)

**Dad**   Will you shut up about going outside! You can't.
**Tony**   Just for a minute.
**Dad**   See that dial on the wall? That tells you how much radiation there still is out there. You'd die.
**Jim Hebden**   We've got to try it sometime.
**Dad**   No one's going outside. We can't, I tell you!
**Uncle Wilf**   Dead – that's what you'd be. Dead!
**Jim**   The food and water in here won't last for ever.
**Aunty Kate**   We've got enough, haven't we, Joan?
**Mum**   I think so. Anyway, they're sure to come and get us soon.
**Linda**   Who'll come and get us? Is there anyone left? After all that bombing?
**Mandy**   Yes. And all the nuclear fall-out.

**Linda**  It's been weeks.
**Mandy**  Too long
**Linda**  Everybody except us is dead.
**Mum**  Don't say that, Linda.
**Uncle Wilf**  You don't know that.
**Mrs Benson**  I'd like to go home soon.
**Uncle Wilf**  She's wandering in her mind. The shock of the bombing finished her.
**Mandy**  I dreamt about being back home last night. Looking out of the back window over the fields. I cried when I woke up.
**Aunty Kate**  Try not to think about it, Mandy.
**Dad**  Give it time. We'll get out.
**Mrs Benson**  The fields were full of mist that morning.
**Uncle Wilf**  Now see what you've done. Started her off again.
**Mrs Benson**  We'd all hired a bus. It was a lovely day. May the seventh.
**Uncle Wilf**  We know.
**Aunty Kate**  You've told us.
**Linda**  Hundreds and hundreds of times.
**Mrs Benson**  The blossom on the trees. You should have seen that blossom.
**Uncle Wilf**  Maybe. But we didn't. That and a lot of other things have gone for good.
**Aunty Kate**  Oh, Wilf!
**Uncle Wilf**  Well, it's right, isn't it? I wish she'd shut up.
**Mrs Benson**  I was sitting next to Jane Wilcox.
**Uncle Wilf**  Who was always so prim and proper.
**Mrs Benson**  That's right. How did you know?
**Uncle Wilf**  Give me strength.
**Mrs Benson**  But in the next seat to us was – what was her name?
**Mum**  Ethel Davey.
**Mrs Benson**  That's right. You weren't there, were you?
**Mum**  How could I be? I wasn't even born then. I'm your next-door neighbour, Joan Swift, Mrs Benson. Don't you know me?
**Mrs Benson**  Oh, yes. We sang on the way back.
**Tony**  It's awfully boring in here.

53

**Dad**  Well, watch telly.
**Tony**  I watched telly all day yesterday. And the day before that.
**Dad**  Watch it again.
**Mum**  Watch one of those video tapes of *Match of the Day*.
**Linda**  Oh, no, not another tape of *Match of the Day*.
**Mandy**  No, Dad.
**Tony**  I know every one of those matches off by heart. And I'm hungry.
**Mum**  We're all hungry. Read a book. Take your mind off it.
**Tony**  I can't. I'm starving. I'd give anything for a hamburger — or an ice-cream.
**Mrs Benson**  We had ice-cream on that day out by the sea.
**Uncle Wilf**  And don't we know it! We know exactly who had what and when. She goes on and on about it. Over and over. I'd like to see her put outside.
**Jim**  That's a rotten thing to say.
**Uncle Wilf**  It wouldn't make any difference to her.
**Jim**  Just because she's old and weak.
**Uncle Wilf**  She eats our food and drinks our water. She doesn't even know what's going on. She's driving me mad.
**Jim**  She's a human being — just like you. She's got as much right to live as the rest of us.
**Uncle Wilf**  She's had her life.
**Jim**  You'd put her out simply because you're younger and stronger. Well — I'm younger and stronger than you. So watch it!
**Uncle Wilf**  Are you threatening me?
**Jim**  I'm only following your lead. Your idea that only the strong should survive is a lousy one. Young Tony's smaller than any of us — what about him?
**Uncle Wilf**  I'm not talking about him. I'm talking about her.
**Jim**  Well — don't!
**Uncle Wilf**  Who do you think you are? You're only here because you had lodgings with her. You're no part of this family. Neither is she. You don't say who comes and goes in this shelter.
**Mum**  And you're not in charge here, Wilf, either. Fancy saying things like that about Mrs Benson!

**Uncle Wilf**  Who is in charge then? You? Don't make me laugh.
**Mum**  This is our shelter and don't you forget it.
**Aunty Kate**  Your shelter! How about all the advice Wilf gave you?
**Mum**  Advice is cheap. All the money came from Ron's building firm.
**Tony**  And Dad did all the work, too.
**Uncle Wilf**  You shut up, you whining little brat! Nobody asked you.
**Tony**  Well — Dad did do all the work.
**Uncle Wilf**  Don't answer me back or I'll clout you!
**Dad**  You won't touch him!
**Uncle Wilf**  Who's going to stop me?
**Dad**  I'll stop you soon enough.
**Uncle Wilf**  I'd just like to see you try.
**Dad**  On your rotten feet, then. I'll show you!

(*The two men are on their feet with their fists clenched*)

**Linda**  Stop it! Stop it! I can't stand it. You said there weren't going to be any more quarrels.
**Mandy**  No. Remember what happened last time.
**Linda**  You could have wrecked the air supply and killed us all.

(*There is a pause.* **Dad** *and* **Uncle Wilf** *stare at each other and then relax*)

**Dad**  I didn't start it.
**Uncle Wilf**  And it wasn't me.
**Aunty Kate**  It was Jim Hebden there.
**Jim**  Maybe it was. I'm sorry. It's the last thing we should do — start another war in here.
**Mum**  It's the strain of it all.
**Aunty Kate**  It's being here and the waiting. Day after day after day. (*She begins to cry*) No one comes.
**Uncle Wilf**  For Heaven's sake, Kate, don't start the waterworks again.
**Aunty Kate**  I can't help it sometimes. (*She pulls herself together*) I'm all right now.

**Dad** Tell you what. Anyone fancy another hand of cards?
**Mum** Not me.
**Uncle Wilf** Not now.
**Linda** No.
**Tony** I wish I could go to a real football match again.
**Uncle Wilf** So do I, son. Eh, Ron?
**Dad** Not half.
**Uncle Wilf** Remember Saturday afternoons?
**Dad** And the pools. Don't forget the pools.
**Uncle Wilf** I'm not. Remember Ben Springer and his form sheets?
**Dad** He tried to make a science of it. He never won anything, though.
**Uncle Wilf** No. I wonder where he is now.
**Dad** I can guess. Poor old Ben.
**Linda** Oh, shut up! Shut up!
**Dad** What's got into you?
**Mandy** You're as bad as Mrs Benson. Both of you. You go on talking about the same old things time after time.
**Linda** Dreaming about the past.
**Mandy** And people like Linda and me — and Tony — we don't have much of a past to dream about.
**Linda** We've got nothing.
**Aunty Kate** You're alive. You've got the telly.
**Uncle Wilf** You've got company. You've got us.
**Mandy** Food, telly and playing card games. What sort of life is that?
**Dad** We're doing our best.
**Linda** It's not enough. I want to walk in the country, see green leaves again, breathe some fresh air.
**Mandy** And hear some different voices.
**Linda** Yes — not just yours, quarrelling all the time.
**Mandy** We'd be better off dead.
**Jim** Don't say that. There's always hope.
**Linda** What can we hope for? No one's going to rescue us.
**Jim** We might try to rescue ourselves.
**Mandy** How? We can't go outside. We're stuck here. Stuck. I hate it. I hate you all.
**Mum** Well! What a thing to say! How ungrateful can you get?

After all your Dad's done for you.
**Linda**  Done? What has he done?
**Mum**  This shelter was his idea in the first place.
**Dad**  And a fat lot of praise I got at the time.
**Mum**  That's true. All the neighbours jeering and laughing while you were building it.
**Uncle Wilf**  But who put you on to solar power and wind power? Where would we have been without the generators?
**Dad**  I grant you that, Wilf. We'd never have done it without you. I never said otherwise.
**Aunty Kate**  So you just leave your elders and betters alone, young Linda.
**Mum**  Where would you have been without us?
**Linda**  We might have been better off. It's people like you who got us here in the first place.
**Uncle Wilf**  What are you talking about?
**Mandy**  You could have done something to stop the war.
**Dad**  How could people like us have stopped a war? It's governments that start wars.
**Linda**  You put the government in power.
**Aunty Kate**  We never wanted a war. It's other countries that start wars.
**Linda**  Is it? It takes two sides to start a war.
**Mandy**  It's people. There's something in human beings that likes fighting. Look at us here — always quarrelling.
**Mum**  That's silly.
**Jim**  Is it? There could be some sense in that.
**Dad**  What do kids know about it?
**Uncle Wilf**  And who asked you to put your oar in anyway?
**Jim**  They're right about some things. You should listen to yourselves talking. Always living in the past.
**Uncle Wilf**  Some people have pleasant memories of the past. What's wrong with that?
**Jim**  It stops you thinking about the future.
**Dad**  We do think of the future.
**Jim**  Do you? It seems to me you spend most of your time blaming each other for the way things are. Blaming and complaining.

57

**Linda**  That's mean. What else can we do being in here but complain?
**Uncle Wilf**  And who gave you the right to criticise?
**Jim**  It's time we started to plan.
**Aunty Kate**  Plan what? We did all the planning of this place. You know so much more about it, don't you?
**Jim**  Sooner or later someone's got to open that door and go out.
**Dad**  No one's said any different, have they?
**Jim**  No one's said much about it, to my mind. And — after we're out — what then?
**Aunty Kate**  There'll be people to tell us what to do.
**Jim**  Will there? Are you sure? We might have to start thinking ahead for ourselves for a change.
**Mandy**  We've got to know it's safe out there before we plan anything else.
**Jim**  And how can we do that unless one of us goes out?
**Tony**  Are we going out?
**Dad**  No, we're not. And you — Jim Hebden — don't start upsetting the kid.
**Uncle Wilf**  I've told you already. You're only here because of our good will.
**Dad**  You don't belong to this family. You've no say.
**Aunty Kate**  When we want to hear from you, we'll ask.
**Dad**  Go out, indeed! It'll be a long time yet. It's suicide out there.
**Uncle Wilf**  So you just keep your trap shut. We'll decide when to go.
**Jim**  All right. Have it your way.

(**Jim** *leaves them and goes over to stand by the door*)

**Uncle Wilf**  Flipping nerve!
**Dad**  We don't need him stirring it.
**Aunty Kate**  Who does he think he is?
**Mum**  Still — someone will have to go out soon.
**Dad**  Don't you start!
**Uncle Wilf**  Don't say you're on his side!
**Mum**  We're running short.
**Dad**  You never said.

**Mum**   I didn't want to worry you. I kept hoping someone would come.
**Mandy**   How short?
**Mum**   There isn't much water and we've only got the soya biscuits left to eat. Two each.
**Uncle Wilf**   Only two?
**Linda**   We could hang on for another week. You can stay alive as long as you've got water.
**Dad**   Maybe. But we'll all be getting weaker and weaker. Tomorrow — or the day after — or the day after that, one of us must go out to look for food.
**Uncle Wilf**   Who?
**Tony**   I'll go.

(*Unseen by any of them,* **Jim** *goes out of the door*)

**Dad**   Don't be a little fool.
**Uncle Wilf**   Linda? You've complained enough about being in here.
**Mum**   Wilf! Send a girl? Why don't you go?
**Uncle Wilf**   We'll have to draw lots for it.
**Dad**   You and I ought to go, Wilf. Then if something happens to one of us, the other might get back.
**Uncle Wilf**   But if we both go, who will look after the women and children?
**Mrs Benson**   Jim? Where's Jim?

(*They all look at the door*)

**Dad**   Jim?

(**Dad** *goes to the door and looks out. Then he comes back*)

**Dad**   He's not there. He's not in the air-lock. He's gone.
**Aunty Kate**   Gone?
**Uncle Wilf**   He's crazy.
**Tony**   No, he's not.
**Linda**   We were hard on him.
**Mandy**   He hasn't gone because of that.
**Dad**   I'll go after him.
**Mum**   No! One man risking his life in that wilderness is enough.

59

**Uncle Wilf**  That's the last of him.
**Aunty Kate**  You would say that!
**Tony**  No! Please let him be safe. Let him come back. I hope he gets back.
**Dad**  So do I, son. God! So do I!

(*They are all silent, looking towards the door*)

## People in the play

1 At the beginning of the play, when asked if there is enough food, Mum says, 'I think so.' Why might she not want to tell them that they are running short?
2 Do you find Mrs Benson irritating or are you sorry for her? Say why you think of her as you do.
3 How long do you think they have been in the shelter? Find some evidence from what the people say in the play to back up your answer.
4 Uncle Wilf calls Tony 'a whining little brat'. Do you agree with this or do you think Tony's behaviour is normal under the circumstances? Give some details from the play to explain your answer.
5 Dad and Uncle Wilf begin to quarrel about Tony. What evidence is there that there have been serious quarrels in the shelter before this?
6 Dad says he can 'guess' what has happened to his old friend Ben Springer. What do you think has happened to Ben?
7 Who seems to be able to stand the strain of being in the shelter better, Mum or Aunty Kate? Explain why you think as you do.
8 Would the shelter have been a success without Uncle Wilf's help in planning or not? Give reasons for your answer.
9 Is Uncle Wilf a coward or is he no worse than most people? Why do you think so?
10 Linda suggests that Jim has left the shelter because they are all unfriendly towards him. Mandy says, 'He hasn't gone because of that.' Why do you think Jim has gone outside? Will he come back if he survives?

## Survival

1 If you had all the money you would ever need and enough over to build a nuclear shelter, would you build yourself one or not? Give reasons for your decision.
2 Uncle Wilf and Jim Hebden start to quarrel over Mrs Benson. Explain what they are quarrelling about. Then say which of them you agree with and why.
3 Who seems to be in charge in the shelter? Would it have been better if there had been just one person whom all the rest obeyed without argument? Explain why you think as you do.

## Writing

1 Will Jim Hebden be safe outside the shelter or will the radiation kill him? If he survives, will he find people to help him and the others? Or will he have to survive without help? If so, will he find food? Where? Will he go back to the others? Will he convince them that they can leave the shelter? Write about what happens next to Jim and the others, either as a story or in the form of a play.
2 Mrs Benson stays happy in the shelter by reliving one marvellous day in her life. Has there been a day like this in your life? Write about it.
3 In the shelter they have food and water, company and television, and they can play card games. Linda says it is not enough. She misses being able to walk in the country. What would you miss most if you had to spend a long time in the shelter? Write about that.

© Paul Groves and Nigel Grimshaw 1983

First published 1983
by John Murray (Publishers) Ltd
50 Albemarle Street, London W1X 4BD

Reprinted 1984 (twice), 1987, 1995

All rights reserved. Unauthorised
duplication contravenes applicable laws.

**British Library Cataloguing in Publication Data**

Groves, Paul
  Six plays for today.
  1. College and school drama
  I. Title    II. Grimshaw, Nigel
  808.2    PN1655

ISBN 0–7195–3998–6

Printed in Hong Kong by
Wing King Tong Co. Ltd